The Official How To Rap Manual

This book is dedicated to Ananzia Hill-West. Your strength and courage is an inspiration to all of us. Thank you to my friends and family. You truly are a gift from GOD without you I don't believe this book would have been completed.

Special Thanks to Big Ro, Al, Marcus "The Young Don", and my baby girl Nel. I love you all.

Table Of Contents

Introduction

Chapter 1

Grammar

Chapter 2

Word Connects and Letter Sounds

Chapter 3

Poetry

Chapter 4

Lyric Writing

Chapter 5

Tone&Pitch

Chapter 6

Music

Chapter 7

Bars and Counts

Chapter 8

Combination Syllables

Introduction

Hello and welcome. What you are about to embark on is one of the most exciting and new beginnings you will love and enjoy for a long time to come. That is unless you are not truly into your art. The levels you will be able to take your rhymes to are unstoppable, unimaginable. This is truly a beginning of many wonderful adventures for you. If you truly are a student of this game and love to practice, write and create wonderful songs using words and phrases. Then this is just what the doctor ordered.

My Name is Jamaal West A.K.A. J-Mill. I came up with this book many years ago. Be sure to visit the website www.how2rap.com. There you will find many new and exciting features. The site is for everyone especially if your a artist producer or model, you should really like the site. If you have any suggestions or questions by all means hola at the kid. Also I have left my email address within these pages so you can contact me at anytime. I will return all emails just make sure you type How To Rap Manual in the subject. I get so many emails a day that I delete those that I think is junk mail. I also have Cd's on the website that you can purchase of me and all the different styles that I laid down from using this manual. Check them out as well. You won't be disappointed because like I said I have been doing this for years so ya boy is far from whack.

I have many different styles but there are so many that haven't been tapped yet. You could be the next to find them. I added some extra pages for you to practice your skills but I would advise you to invest in a notebook so you can practice your rhymes in. I have at least 50-60 of these laying around from front to back. This book was actually written in one of them. But enough about me. I truly hope you enjoy this for many years to come. Now lets begin.

This is it, the first ever of its kind. Drum roll please. And without further a due I would like to introduce..."**The Official How To Rap Manual**". With this manual you will learn to make songs you never believed you could make. You will take your rhyme skill to heights unimaginable. With **The Official How To Rap Manual** you have the potential to take your rhymes to a level you never believed you could. You will be putting together rhyme schemes you never knew existed. Only a person with greed would want these for their self. This one book could make you millions in the music biz. Or at least a million rhymes and then with the right connections then. You get the picture.

In this remarkable creation you will learn about consonants, poetry, phrases, and pronouns etc. to take your rap game to a whole new level. That's just a few of the things you will learn in this wonderful opportunity. Be the wittiest with the most vocabulary or with styles that most people never even heard before. Now is the time if you are truly serious about becoming a student of this game.

One thing I learned about this game or
life in general and that is time waits
for no one. So you gotta get it when you
can. Feel me?

Break out your rap book and your
Instrumental CD(Also available at
www.how2rap.com) and begin to see the
unbelievable potential of **"The Official
How To Rap Manual"**.

In the following two chapters you
will learn about word sounds and grammar.
This information is very important in
your quest for knowledge in this game of
rhyme and reason. Communication plays a
big part in Hip-Hop so one of the most
important things that you will need to
create in your lyrics is wordplay so lets
start with grammar.

Chapter 1

Grammar

The information in these first two chapters can be found in any dictionary.... Well almost any dictionary. I actually had to put some work in to put this book together. This book has been in the making since 1994. That's the year when I began to take my craft as an artist seriously, and making plans for the future to help other artist improve their art. I stumble on to this idea only because at the time when I first started rapping in 1986, I didn't have a book of some sort, or anything that I could study from to help make me a better mcee. So that is how the book began. Back in '86 it was just putting words together and saying them over a beat trying to imitate my favorite rappers, Sugar Hill Gang, Big Daddy Kane, and Curtis Blow to name a few. These were the Jay Z''s Pac's''s and Biggie's of the Late 80's early 90's. Mainly these two chapters were put together for you as the artist to study. Come back to these pages time and time again until the information they possess on them are embedded in your brain. Okay lets begin with consonant clusters.

Now a consonant cluster is a group of consonants which have no intervening vowel(**a,e,i,o,u** and sometimes **y**). For example the word **splits** has two consonants clusters **SPL** and **TS**. **SPL** is what we will classify as an initial consonant cluster(this just means the consonant cluster that is in the beginning of a word). **SPL** which we depict with the letter **S** followed by a hyphen (Hyphen shows where words are either in front of or behind of) **S-**. For example a hyphen followed by a k (**-K**) would look like **SK** or a **T** followed by a hyphen (**T-**) would look like **TR**. Basically just replace a letter or letters in place of the hyphen. That was easy right?

We deal with two main categories of the initial consonants and they are **Regular** and **Irregular**. Regular clusters are **-L -R** and **S-**. There are 8 irregular consonants that we will be concentrating on. View **Fig 1**.

Now focus your attention to **Fig 1a**. These are the final consonant clusters. These are the last group of consonants in a word which have no intervening vowels (**a,e,i,o,u** and sometimes **y**). For example the final consonant in **swarm**. Would be **rm**, and we would show this by using a hyphen in front of **RM** (**-RM**). Remember the hyphen shows where the cluster in question relates to the word. The ones shown in Figure 1a are the most common used.

Initial Consonant Clusters

Regular   **Irregular**

-L	-R	S-	Cont	dw
bl	br	sc	sph	sw
cl	cr	sk	spl	tw
fl	dr	sch	spr	qu
gl	fr	scr	str	squ
pl	gr	sm	tr	st
sl	pr	sn	thr	shr
	scr	sp		x

Fig 1

Final Consonant Clusters

-CT	-ST	-NK	-LM	-TCH	-RK -RT
-FT	-LP	-SK	-NG	-LB	-RL
-LT	-MP	-LD	-CK	-LGE	-RM
-NT	-SP	-LK	-LL	-RGE	-RN
-PT	-ND	-LF	-SH	-RD	-RP

Fig 1a

Next we will talk about **Lax Vowels** and **Tense Vowels**. These basically play a big part in the sound produced by your vocal chords. Lax vowels are vowels that leave your vocal chords and tongue relaxed. Hence lax vowels. Can you guess what tense vowels do? That's correct. Tense vowels are vowels that leave your vocal chords and tongue tense. See *Figure 2* we used colors to show those vowels that sound alike (However if you have one of the earlier editions you will only see black and white-tight budget).

Lax Vowels leave vocal chords and tongue relaxed.
Color Scheme shows alike sounds.

i splint	**augh** caught	**i** easily	**air** chair
a damage	**ough** thought	**e** system	**are** dare
ei counterfeit	**aw** law	**a** alone	**ear** wear
y sympathetic	**oa** broad	**oo** hood, crook	
e spent, swell	**u** put, pull	**er** term	
ea dead	**ou** touch, could	**ur** turn	
a blast	**u** chunk, putt	**ir** thirsty	
o blond, **o** lost	**o+e** love	**eir** their	

9

au fault   **o** gallop **ere** there

Fig. 2

Tense Vowels require movement of the vocal chords. *Color Scheme shows alike sounds.*

Pronounced by name

i+e stripe,glide machine	**ee** queen	**o+e** store,stroke
ia diamond,trial	**ey** key	**oa** road
ia serial	**a+e** plane	**ou** soul
ie tie, field	**ey** obey	**oe** toe
igh high, flight	**y** city	**ow** snow
e+e even, theme	**ai** praise	**u+e** crude
y reply	**ay** decay	**ue** argue
ea each, scream	**eigh** eight,weigh	**ui** fruit
	ea steak	

Fig. 2 cont

Not pronounced by name *Color Scheme shows alike sounds*

ie achieve	**eu** feud, neutral	**ou** soup
oi voice	**ew** jewels	
oy annoy	**oo** boot	
ou amount	**ui** bruise	
ow down	**ue** blue	

Fig. 2 cont

Taking this procedure one step further *Figure 2a* shows vowels influenced by **R** and **L**.

Vowels influenced by R

ar bar	**ir** stir
aer	**or** for
er her	**ur** fur
eer deer	

Vowels influenced by L

al final

el infidel

ial social

le battle

Fig. 2a

Okay now that you got the vowel sounds down. Lets take another look at consonants. *Figure 3* shows every possible way consonants are used in the English language. Each consonant is put in parenthesis **( )** and followed by an example of the word that shows the sound of that actual consonant. For example the consonant **(ch)** sounds like the **Ch** in <u>Ch</u>ief. Under each consonant in parenthesis is followed by alike sounds. Another example of this is the **(ch)** sound in <u>chief</u> has **si** in it's category because the **si** in *mansion* has that **(Ch)** sound in it. Got it? Good. Now lets move on to suffixes.

Consonant

(b)b bed	**(g)g** give	**(l)l** live	**(r)r** red	**(t)t** toe
bb bubble	**gg** egg	**ll** call	**rh** rhythm	**ed** talked
(ch)ch chief	**gh** ghost	**(m)m** more	**rr** carrot	**ght** bought
si mansion	**gu** guard	**lm** calm	**wr** wrong	**tt** bottom
su conscious	**wh** who	**mm** hammer	**(s)s** see	**c** center
ti question	**(j)j** just	**(n)n** not	**ce** nice	**(th)th** thin
tu natural	**du** graduate	**gn** gnat	**ci** city	**th** then
(d)d do	**dg** judgment	**kn** knife	**ps** psycho	**(v)v** visit
dd ladder	**di** soldier	**nn** runner	**sc** scene	**(w)w** well
(f)f feed	**ge** page	**pn** pneumatic	**ss** mess	**wh** where
				(y)y yet

(zh)zi brazier
ge garage
su measure
si division
zu azure

ff muffin	gi gin	(ng)ng ringing	(sh)sh ship	i union
ft soften	(k)k keep	nk pink	ci special	(z)s has
gh tough	c car	(p)p pen	ss tissue	se rise
ph physics	cc account	pp supper	ssi mission	zz buzzard
.	ch character		ti fictitious, caption	z zone
.	ck back			

Fig. 3

A suffix is a **word ending** and Prefixes are **word beginnings**. <u>Suffixes and Prefixes are group of letters that are added to the beginning or ending of a root word</u>. A root word is a word that stands on its own. By adding beginnings (Prefixes) and endings(Suffixes) to root words, new words can be made. For example the root word **comfort** can become a new word by adding the Prefix (beginning) "**dis**". **Dis***comfort*. Adding the suffix(ending) "**able**", **comfort** becomes *comfort***able**. **Figure 4** shows a few suffixes that you can study from.

Note: inflections are the patterns of stress and intonation in a language. In other words alteration in pitch and or tone of the voice. They can also be defined as the change in the formal word. For a complete list of suffixes and prefixes please refer to the back of the book.

Suffixes indicating inflections

Tense	Number	Comparison
-ing	-s	-er
-ed	-es	-est
	-n	

Suffixes indicating parts of speech

Nouns	Adverbs	Verbs	Adjective
tion station	**ly** suddenly	**ize** colonize	**ant**distant
ment statement	**ally**	**ate** operate	**ent** apparent
ity security		**fy** electrify	**al** typical
sion decision		**en** cheapen	**ful** careful
ness kindness			**less** careless
ance insurance			**ic** basic
ence sequence			**ish** stylish
ency			**ine**
ture picture			**ous** generous
al			**able** capable
y property			**ible** reversible
ist			**i've** extensive
ory memory			**ary** ordinary
ing opening			
cy tendency			

Fig. 4

Next we will look at Nouns. Nouns are defined as a **person**, **place**, **thing**, **animal**, and **abstract idea**. See **Fig. 5** All sentences have nouns so it is safe to say every Rhyme has a noun in it.

Johnny, mailman, dog, Maryland are all examples of nouns

There are many type of nouns.
For example:

Noun Genders-are nouns that can refer to men or women like **coach, teacher,** or **engineer** to name a few.

Plural Nouns- are nouns that change their form to show number. This is done by adding "**-s**"or "**-es**".

truth/truths and **box/boxes**

Possessive Nouns– Show possession of a noun by adding an apostrophe'

> **Carmen's** bag or I can't stop the **dogs'** barking.

Proper Nouns–are always written with a capital letter.

> **N**ew **Y**ork, **T**immy

Common Nouns– are nouns used in the general sense and are the opposite of proper nouns, meaning they never get capitalized unless in the beginning of a sentence.

> **garden/town/miles**

Abstract nouns–name anything you can not relate to in the physical senses.

> **Justice/childhood/afterthought**

Collective Nouns– name a group of **things, animals,** or **persons.**

> **jury/flock/class**

And last but not least Pronouns. These are substitutes for nouns. See **Fig. 5** for examples.

Pronouns (Substitutes for nouns**)**

> **"Mary said <u>she</u> was going"**
> **"The men forget <u>their</u> tickets"**
> **"The officer blew <u>his</u> whistle"**

Commonly used Pronouns

I	he	them	any	another	anyone
my	his	which	both	anybody	
mine	him	what	each	everybody	
me	she	who	either	nobody	

```
we      her     whose   nether   somebody
our     hers    whom    few      no one
ours    it      this    many     someone
us      its     that    none     everyone
you     they    these   some     one
yours   their   those   several  whoever
your    theirs  all     other    whosoever
```

Fig. 5

The remaining of this chapter explains other grammar usage that is critical to your development as an emcee. Read and study the rest of this chapter. You will definitely be incorporating grammer into your rhymes. So be sure to study the chapter thoroughly.

Verbs

-Verbs make a statement about the subject. Most *verbs* express action.

"The hunter ***shot*** the deer"   "I ***pricked*** my finger"   "The manager ***wrote*** a letter"

-Another group of verbs that do not show action is the verb(to be). Common forms of this verb are (are, is, was, and, were). These are called **linking verbs**. Because they link words together in a sentence.

"Mother ***is*** happy" (**really means happy mother**)

-Verb phrases are verbs of two or more words. The verb form at the end of the verb phrase is always the principle verb (action), the other forms are the *Auxiliary/helping verbs*.

-The men ***are*** working in the fields.

-The men ***have been*** working.

-The men ***must have been*** working.

Commonly used auxiliary verbs

am	have	do	should
is	has	did	must
are	had	does	should have
was	have been	may	would have
where	had been	can	must have
will be	has been	might	should have been
shall be	shall	could	could have been
could be	will	would	must have been

Adjectives

-Are describing words usually adding new ideas to nouns and pronouns.

-Are also referred to as modifiers because they describe, limit, or restrict the meaning in anyway.

-**a**, **an**, and **the** are adjectives but in grammar are called articles.

> **The** (definite article)
> **a/an** (indefinite articles)

Adjectives modifying-nouns

long road **good** friend   **rainy** day

rusty nail   **worthy** cause   **rapid** typist

old piano **steep** hill   **essential** parts

Adverbs

-Are also modifiers

-are added to verbs to modify or expand the meaning of verbs

-may also modify adjectives other adverbs

-usually answer the question (when, where, in what manner, to what extent/degree) also (time/place) "sometimes, everywhere"

> "You must shred up the copy **now**"
> "we put the desk **there**"
> "Mary walked **gracefully**"

Function Words

-Same words are used as different parts of speech.

The *light(n.)* in my study is poor
Please *light(n.)* the candles

Father is a *fast(adj.)* driver
Father drives to *fast(adv.)*

Prepositions

-Shows relationships between certain words in a sentence.

The accident occurred *on* the bridge (*preposition*)

on the bridge (*prepositional phrase*)

The accident occurred *under* the bridge (*preposition*)

The accident occurred *near* the bridge (*preposition*)

The accident occurred *above* the bridge (*preposition*)

Commonly used Prepositions

above	at	by	into	toward
about	before	down	like	through

across	behind	during	near	under
after	below	except	of	until
against	beneath	for	off	up
along	beside	from	on	upon
among	between	in	since	with
around	beyond	inside	to	within

Conjunctions

-Joins words or groups of words

"Mark drives to fast *and* too recklessly"
(joins two adverbs)

"He *or* I will audit the account"
(joins two pronouns)

"I fell *and* broke my arm" (Joins two verbs)

"It is a large *but* attractive home"
(Joins two Adjectives)

Interjections   (Exclamatory words)

-Express strong feeling or sudden emotion.
Nouns, pronouns, adjectives, and other parts of
speech are often used as interjections.

"*Heavens*! I cut my finger"

"*Good*! I'm glad to hear that."

The Noun parts of speech consists of 8 groups.

-Nouns are

Persons   (*Soldier*, *Jane*, *friend*)
Substances (*iron*, *air*, *water*, *food*)

Animals   (*Elephant*, *Mouse*, *Zebra*)
Qualities (*kindness*, *heroism*, *beauty*)

Places   (*Home, Chicago, camp*)
Actions   (*climbing, cooking, reading*)
[**Things**]**Objects** (*desk, picture, computer*)
Measures (*year, pound, inch, day*)

"The *Soldier* is wearing his new uniform"

"*Chicago* is a great industrial *city*"

"*Iron* is awful metal"

That concludes this chapter. Be sure to study this chapter. You will come back time and time again. I promise you. Now we are going to move on to chapter 2. We will be dealing with word connects and letter sounds. This will come in handy as well so step it up.

Chapter 2

Word connects and letter sounds

Okay looking good. Now lets begin with Chapter 2. Hopefully by now you are beginning to understand the importance of grammar and parts of speech in your music. Now in this chapter you will learn how parts of speech are combined to make word sounds. Study these examples and techniques just as you did in Chapter 1. These are self explanatory. So what are you waiting for? Get to it.

Lets look at consonants and vowel combinations. When a word ends with a consonant and then is followed by a word that begins with a vowel, that sound is portrayed by mixing the consonant with the vowel, making two words into one.

For example:

Consonant and Vowel (Semivowels **W, Y, R**)

<u>Big up</u> to my niggaz / **Bi gup** to my niggaz

Notice how words ending with a consonant followed by a word beginning with a vowel sounds coming out of your mouth. Big up actually sounds like Bi gup when you say it. Applying this into your rhymes will make words sound more fluent when you spitting that fire. This rule should work with all words formed in this way. Test it out.

Now this is a nice little practice to use. Pay attention to the way consonants are expressed through your mouth. This is good to know. Try incorporating bars that just have consonants that roll off the lips or behind the teeth like the examples below. This shows how certain consonants play within the mouth.

Lips: **P**erfect **F**or / **B**ig **V**enus
Behind Teeth: **T**o **Ch**ase **S**ome **Sh**orty / **D**on't **J**ust **Z**ip **Zh**ur
Throat: **K**eep **H**aving / **G**irls Tho**ng**s **R**eady

When a word ending in a vowel is followed by a word beginning with a vowel, notice the letter sound that is produced.

Vowel and Vowel (W/Y)

You **(w)** were   I **(y)** am

Other examples of word connections and letter sounds are:

T and Y = CH   Can't**+y**ou do it

D and Y = J   What di**d+y**ou do

S and Y(u) = SH   Insurance/ Mis**s+y**ou

Z and Y(u) = J   Casual/How**s+y**our family

   (Length, Pitch, Clarity)

These are the ways to stress a syllable. They are length(Similar to Pac and Biggie's flow), Pitch(Also used by (Pac) and clarity(Similar to Jigga and Big). Pac uses lengthy syllables in his rhymes like in Dear Momma "And though you was a crack <u>Pheeeeen</u> momma" and Biggie's

Back in the Day "Remember back in the daaaays when niggaz had waaaaives." The Official Hip-Hop Manual shows lengthy syllables with a underline under the word or syllable that is length stressed. For example. In Big's rhyme we would write it like "Remember back in the days when niggaz had waives." More examples of this are shown at the end of this chapter. I will take a verse from 3 of my most favorite emcees Biggie, Pac, and Jay-Z.

Pitch is shown either high pitch or low pitch. High pitch is shown with a parenthesis over the word (sort of like a mountain covering the word) and low pitch is shown with a parenthesis under the word. Example of this is shown below.

(T is T)

If **T** is at the beginning of a word it is a strong clear **T** sound.

-beginning of a word (**T**able, **T**omorrow)

-stressed **T** combinations (**ST, TS, TR, CT, LT, NT**)

-in the past tense **D sounds like T** after unvoiced consonants (**F, K, P, S, CH, SH, TH**)
Trapp**ed**/Wish**ed**

(T is D)

In the middle of a word **T is D**

-Get a (Gedda), Better (Bedder), Water (Wawder), Heater (Heeder), Letter (Ledder)

(T is silent)

When **T and N** are so close **T is silent**

-Interview (Innerview), Advantage (Avanage),

If T is at the end of a word you almost don't hear it at all (Sho**t**, Wha**t**) "Tha**t**'s qui**t**e righ**t** isn'**t** i**t**"

(T is held)

With **tain**, **tten** and some **NT** the **T is held**

-Wri**tten**, Cer**tain**, Forgo**tten**, Sen**t**ence

(I and E)

If final consonant is unvoiced (**t, k, f, p, s, sh, ch**) then the middle vowel sound is quick and sharp

-Bit / beet

If final consonant is voiced (**d, g, v, b, z, zh, j**) or any vowel then the middle vowel sound is doubled

-bi-id / bee-eed

Notice below parenthesis show actual sound.

-[**S**] is pronounced after the voiceless consonants.

     p keeps   **f** laughs

     t hates   **th** paths

k seeks

-[**Z**] after voiced consonants, .and after all vowels(**a, e, o, u,** and sometimes **y**) *"pays"*

b robes   **v** loves

d needs   **th** bathes

g tags   **m** homes

l balls   **n** fines

r hears   **ng** sings

-[**IZ**] after consonant sounds

s faces   **sh** wishes **ch** watches

z rises   **zh** beige **j** pages

-[**T**] after voiceless consonants

p helped **f** laughed **s** faced

k poked   **th** bathed **sh** wished

ch watched

-[**D**] after voiced consonants and all vowels(**a, e, o, u,** and sometimes **y**) *"paid"*

b stabbed **th** bathed **m** roamed **l** called

g begged **z** praised **n** rained **r** cared

v saved   **j** paged   **g** banged

-[**ID**] after consonant sounds

d needed **t** wanted

C followed by **e, i** or **y** usually has the soft sound of "**s**"

cyst / central / city

G followed by **e, i** or **y** usually has soft sound of "**j**"

gem / gym / gist

When a syllable ends in a consonant and has only one vowel, that vowel is short

f**a**t / b**e**d / f**i**sh / sp**o**t / l**u**ck

When a syllable ends in a silent "**e**", the silent "**e**" is a signal that the vowel in front of it is long.

m**a**ke / f**e**te / k**i**te / r**o**pe / **u**se

Besides diphthongs when a syllable has 2 vowels together, the first vowel is usually long and the second is silent.

P**ai**n, **ea**t, b**oa**t, res/c**ue**, s**ay**, gr**ow**

When a syllable ends in any vowel and is the only vowel, that vowel is usually long.

P**a**/per, m**e**, **I**, **o**/pen, **u**/nit, and m**y**

When a vowel is followed by an "**r**" in the same syllable, that vowel is "r-controlled". It is not long nor short. R-controlled "**er, ir,** and **ur**" often sound the same (like "**er**") "t**er**m, s**ir**, f**ir**, f**ur**, f**ar**, f**or**, su'g**ar**, or/d**er**"

Okay now lets focus on accent rules. Accents are important because a lot of the times you can rhyme accents. For example see how I try to rhyme using aye accent through out this line (underline shows aye accent) "no need to complain the way the game makes a nigga lose faith."

Accent Rules

-Accents are often on the **first syllable**

    Ba/sic, **pro**/gram

-In words that have **suffixes** or **prefixes** the accent is usually on the main root word

    Box/es, un/**tie**

-Two *vowel* letters together in the **last syllable** of a word often indicates an accented last syllable.

    Com/**plain,** con/**ceal**

-When there are two like consonant letters within a word, the syllable before the double consonant is usually consonant.

    Be/gi**n**/**n**er, let/**t**er

-The accent is usually on the syllable before the suffixes **-ion, ity**, **-ic**, **-ical**, **-ian**, **-ial**, or **-ious,** and on the second syllable before the suffix -**ate.**

    Af/fec/ta'/**tion**, dif/fer/en'ti/**ate**

-In words of three or more syllables, one of the first two syllables is usually accented.

    Ac/**ci**/dent, **de**/**ter**'/mine

      Next we're going to take a look at using tone in phrases. This is important because a rappers tone on certain bars

can enhance songs incredibly. Practice
your lines in different tone and see if
you can tell the difference.

     Dogs eat _Bones_

First half usually sets up second half

    Dogs eat _Bones_, but _Cats_ eat _Fish_

When you want to preface your statement use rising
tone.

    As we all _know_, _dogs_ eat _bones_

All but the last item in a list have a rising
tone.

    Dogs eat _bones_, _kibbles_ and _meat_

Regular question goes up but drops back down at
end.

    Do _dogs_ eat _bones_?

Repeated rhetorical, emotional question goes up
and then up again at the end.

    Do _dogs_ eat _bones_?!!

To emphasize one thing over another reflect the
contrast with pitch change

    Bob studies _English_

    Bob _studies_ English, but he doesn't _use_ it

Nouns carry new info. and the stress in a
sentence.

    The verses below are examples from 3 of my
favorite emcees. The examples will give you a

better understanding of how **"The Official How To Rap Manual"** shows bar counting, combinations, and how easy it is to get the format down when writing your music. If you would like for me to break down any other artists verses or verses for you please contact me at staff@how2rap.com. Or just visit www.how2rap.com and leave me a message and we may be able to throw it up on the site. There is a key at the beginning showing the meaning behind certain symbols that will be good to know when your writing your rhymes. With that said we are at the end of this chapter. Next we will look at poetry. Study this chapter intensely because if your a rapper, singer etc. you are a poet. No if ands or buts. You are a poet. So be sure to focus and study the next chapter.

Underline	_____	Shows the beginning of singy syllables, also shows group rhyming (takin my life, while i was makin time trife.
Upside Downside Parenthesis	Don't Play	Shows Loudness and extremely low sounding of a word.
Dash	_____	Shows continuation from one bar to the next. (Means you don't show any hesitation from bar to bar)
Slash	/	Shows pause between or within bars
Comma	,	Shows short pause between or within bars.
Point	●	When over a word in rhyme shows where that word is placed within bars. Can either be secondary or primary count. Always even 2,4,6, or 8.

Underline	_____	Shows the beginning of singy syllables, also shows group rhyming (takin my life, while i was makin time trife.
Bold	**Bold**	Shows main rhyming words within bars
Italic	*Italic*	Shows other rhyme words besides primary rhyme words. Usually shows inner rhymed words.

Note: 32 points equal 16 bars. Notice Pac's
verse on points 26 and 28 (bars 13&14) they are
set a little ways off of the word. This is
because the words do not fall exactly on that
point. It is like a half second before the point.
Listen to this verse and you'll catch it. The Pac
example has them through out the verse. Can you
find them? Also notice Big's verse on points 26
(bar 13). The one with the dash. This dash shows
continuation from one bar to the next. The key
above is helpful so be sure to study from that in
the future.

Artist: Notorious B.I.G.

Album: Ready to Die

Song: Juicy

Verse Three:

Super Nintendo *Sega* **Genesis**

When I was *dead broke* man I couldn't **picture this**

50 *inch screen* money green leather **sofa**

Got two rides a *limousine* with a **chauffeur**

Phone bill about two G's **flat**

No need to worry my accountant handles **that**

And my whole crew is **loungin'**

Celebratin' every day no more public **housin'**

Thinkin' **back** on my one-room **shack**

Now my mom pimps a **Ac'** with minks on her **back**

And she loves to show me off of **course**

Smiles every time my face is up in The **Source**

We used to **fuss** when the landlord *dissed* **us-**

No heat, wonder why *Christmas missed* **us**

Birthdays was the **worst days**

Now we sip champagne when we **thirst-ay**

Uh, damn *right* I *like* the *life* I **live**

'Cause I went from **negative** to **positive** And it's all...

Artist: 2Pac

Album: All Eyez on Me

Song: I Ain't Mad At ya

Verse One:

Now we was once two ni..z of the **same kind**
Quick to holla at a hoochie with the **same line**
You was just a little smaller but you still **roll**
Got stretched to Y.A. and hit the hood **swoll**
Member when you had a jheri curl *didn't quite learn*
On the *block* witcha *glock* **trippin off sherm**
Collect calls to the till, sayin how ya **changed**
Oh you a Muslim now, no more dope **game**
Heard you might be comin home, just got **bail**
Wanna go to the Mosque don't wanna chase **tail**
I seems I lost my little homie he's a **changed man**
Hit the *pen and* now no *sinnin* is the **game plan**
When I talk about money all you see is the **struggle**
When I tell you I'm livin large you tell me it's **trouble**
Congratulation on the **weddin**, I hope your wife know
She got a playa for life, and that's no bullsh..in
I know we grew apart, you probably don't **remember**
I used to fiend for your sister but never went up **in her**
And I can see us after school we'd **BOMB-**
on the first motherfu..r with the **wrong** s..t on
Now the whole s..t's changed, and we don't even **kick it-**
Got a big money scheme, and you ain't even **with it**
Hmm, knew in my heart you was the same motherf..er **bad**
Go toe to toe when it's time for roll you got a **brother's back**
And I can't even trip, cause I'm just *laughin at cha*
You tryin hard to maintain then go head-
cause I ain't **mad at cha** (Hmm, I ain't mad at cha)

Artist: Jay-Z

Album: The Blue Print

Song: Song Cry

[Verse 1]

Good dude, I know you love me like **cooked food**
Even though a nigga got **move** like a **crook move**
We was together on the block since **free lunch**
We shoulda been together havin 4 **Seasons brunch**
We used to use umb*rellas* to face the bad **weather**
So now we travel first **class** to change the fore**cast**
Never in **bunches,** just me and *you*-
I loved your point of *view* cause you held no **punches**
Still I left you for months on **end**
It's been months since I checked back **in**
Were somewhere in a **small town**, somewhere lockin'm **all**
down
Woodgrain four and *change* Armor **All'd down**
I can understand why you want a di**vorce now**
Though I can't let you **know it**, pride won't let me **show**
it
Pretend to be her**oic** that's just one to **grow with**
But deep inside a nigga **so sick**

Chapter 3

Poetry

Now in this chapter we are going to talk about poetry. In this chapter you will learn the terms and different styles of poetry that will have and impact in your ability to write songs. You can use some of these forms of poetry in a whole song or you can incorporate different ones through out the song all together. A lot of or at least all artist use these forms in their rhymes styles. From Biggie to Jay-Z. Even Singers and Rock'N'Roll artists use these forms in their music. So be sure to focus and study the following terms. You may already be incorporating the basics in your rhymes but just do not know the terms. I can almost guarantee it. Some of the terms without examples can easily be found by typing the term in a search engine on the Internet. If you need help just email me (staff@how2rap.com) and I will help you find it.

Repetition of **sounds, syllables, words, phrases, lines, stanzas** or **metrical patterns, word endings, identical syllables** are all a basic device in poetry.

Masculine Ending is a line ending in a stressed syllable.

(~ -) **ex.** something there is that....love a **wall**

Feminine Ending is a line ending in a unstressed syllable.

(- ~) **ex.**   like to the lark….of day ri**sing**

- **stressed**   ~ unstressed

- Monosyllabic   fiend   ~ -   Iamb To-day

~   unstressed   Hit   - ~   Trochee Dai-ly

- - Spondee   Day-Break   - ~ ~ Dactyl Yes-ter-day

~ ~ Pyrrhic   fast-food   ~ ~ - Anapest In-ter-vene

(1) Syllable   (2) Syllable   (3) Syllable

- stressed   ~ - iamb   ~ ~ - anapest   ~ ~ ~ tribach

~ unstressed - ~ trochee   - ~ ~ dactyl   - - -   molossus

                 ~ ~ pyrrhic   ~ - ~ amphibrach ~ - -   bacchic

-                - spondee   - ~ - cretic   - - ~   antibacchic

(4) Syllable

~ ~ ~ ~ proceleusmatic - ~ ~ ~ 1st person ~ - - - 1st epitrite - ~ - ~ ditrochee

- - - -   dispondee   ~ - ~ ~ 2nd person - ~ - - 2nd epitrite ~ - ~ - di-iamb

~ - - ~   antipast   ~ ~ - ~ 3rd person - - - ~ 3rd epitrite ~ - - ~ major iomic

- ~ ~ -   choriamb   ~ ~ ~ - 4th person - - - ~ 4th epitrite ~ ~ - - minor iomic

Homophones are words that sound the same but have different meanings and spellings.

(ad / add, allowed / aloud, etc.)

Acrostic poem has the initial letters of the lines read downward spelling out a name or passage.

Alliterative Meter is a line with 4 stresses.

> He **through** the **thickest** of the **throng** gun **theste**

Alphabet Poem (abecedarius) is arranged according to the alphabet.

Chance Poetry is drawing words from a card and picking them at random to furnish a poem

> **Ex.**   opening dictionary and word picking.

Echo Verse is the last syllable or two, of a main line perhaps with different spelling or meaning.

Alliteration is repetition of consonant sounds.

> -Beginning of words (**R**oof / **R**ighteous :**r**)
>
> -End of words   (Thic**k** / Cree**k**   :**k**)
>
> -Parallel (or cross) (**B**ig **t**ime /**B**us **T**rip:**b,t**)
>
> -Middle   (Ru**nn**er / Fla**nn**el   :**nn**)
>
> -Unstressed   (mail**b**ox / Caro**b**   :**b**)
>
> -Reversal   (**Taw**ny / Aeron**aut**ics   :t, aw)

Enjambment is a line that continues to the next line connecting.

Anadiplosis is repetition of the last word or phrase at the beginning of the next line.

> **Ex.** ·Flowers in a **basket**

Basket on the **bed**

Bed in the **chamber**

Chamber in the house

Anaphora is repetition of the first word or phrase at the beginning of successive lines.

> **Ex.** **By** our first…….
>
> **By** all…………...
>
> **By** our long…….

Anastrophe is inversion of natural word order.

Ex. "**His Golden locks,** *Time hath to silver turn.*" Natural word order would be "*Time hath turned* **his Golden locks** *to silver.*"

Antimeablole is repetition of words in a phrase in reverse order.

> **Ex.** "I should *eat to live* not *live to eat.*"

Antithesis is conflicting ideas usually arranged in parallel structure.

> **Ex.** what we *gained in skill* we *lost in strength.*

Polyptoton is repetition of words derived from the same root

> **Ex.** *conception / conceive*

Polysyndeton is repetition of conjunctions, such as *and.*

Ex. *And* the earth…, *and* darkness, *and* void.

Anthimeria is the substitution of one part of speech for another.

Onomatopoeia is word sounds that imitate the sense.

(*plop, boom, screech,* etc.)

Oxymoron is contradicting word combinations.

(*happy* **sorrow**, *big* **small**)

Pun is word play.

3 types

  -**Antanclasis** is repetition of a word in different senses

  (If we don't <u>*hang*</u> *together* we'll <u>*hang*</u> *separately*)

  -**Paranomasia** is word alike in sound but different in meaning.

   (*red / read*)

  -**Line** is a visual stretch of words. **5 ways to make a line.**

    -Using regular meter requiring a set number of syllables and stresses accumulating before line ends

    -Ending line on a rhyme word

    -Following a cadence, an unmeasured surge of rhythm.

-choosing line length visually making it either similar to near by lines or different.

-Imposing line breaks where a pause occurs or between words usually grouped together (prepositional phrases)

Cento is a poem composed of passages taken from another poet.

Rhopalic are lines that consist of each word having one more syllable than the last.

"*I disdain Phopalic composition*" Can also go in opposite direction.

Holorhyming Verse is a line where every syllable must rhyme.

Permutational lines can be read in any order

Tautogram is text when each word begins with the same letter.

      Ex. Alphabetical **A**frica

Haikuzation poet keeps the rhyming part of a poem but gets rid of the rest.

Ex. Never *take* / any *natural thing* / *make* / *enameling* / *awake.* / *sing* / of Byzantium / *to come*

-**Alternating Qua** – *abab*

-**Envelope Qua** – *abba*

-**Even Rhyme Qua** – *XaXa* (*aXaX*)

38

-2 and 4 rhyme 1 and 3 do not (1 and 3 rhyme 2 and 4 do not)

-Mono Rhyme – *aaaa*

Rhymes differ according to the number of syllables that are echoed.

Perfect rhyme falls on a *single stress.*

    (I rise *hair* / And I.... *air*)

Polysyllabic words can also be part of stress.

    (In *sea* / deep *vanity*) Poets tend to place monosyllabic words before polysyllabic words.

2 Syllable words consisting of a stressed and then unstressed syllable are also used for rhyme sounds.

    (*thicken* / *quicken*)

Triple Rhyme is 3 syllable words.

    (*gunnery* / *nunnery*)

Assonant Rhyme has the same vowel sound but the final consonant is different.

    (g*ate* / s*ake*)

Alliterative or Double Consonant Rhyme is when the vowel is different but the surrounding consonants are the same.

Rhyming on a weak syllable of a 2 syllable word.

    (flower / tatter, slimy / gravy)

Apocopated Rhyming is rhyming part of a multi syllabic word with the final syllable of another.

(*seizure / freeze*)

Wrenched Rhyme is *misspelling/pronouncing* or *garbled* in some way to rhyme with another word.

(*rhinoceros / perpocerous*)

Diminishing Rhyme is losing or gaining consonants as words are repeated.

(*Charm / Harm / Arm*)

Broken Rhyme is when one of the rhyme sounds is the first part of a hyphenated word.

(parenthe*sis* / *lis*-some)

Rhythm in metrical poetry resembles the way melody plays around the *steady beat rising*, *falling*, *slowing down*, *speeding up*, and *pausing*.

The number of syllables per line, normally ten, could be nine and sometimes eight, and as many as twelve but never to fewer or more than that.

-**near rhymes** – *dress / pressed*

-**eye rhyme** – *wind* (**n.**) / *kind*

-**assonance** – *tank / last*

-**consonance** – *bad / good*

-**alliteration** – *fellow / freaks*

Internal rhyme- **ex.** and the priests in black *gowns* were making there *rounds*.

Exact rhyme – *wits / hits*
(**masculine** 1syllable) *Sorrow / to-morrow*
(**feminine** 2 syllable second stress)

Slant (near/half) rhyme – *ground / mind*
(**masculine**)

>   *December / grisamber*
(**feminine**)

Mosaic rhyme – has to have at least 2 syllables
but can have 3 or 4 possibly even more.

Ex. (*intellectual / hen-pecked you all*)

**also is when one word with more than one
syllable is rhymed with identical amounts of
single syllable words.**

>   (*Prided / I did*)

Wrenched rhyme – is a word being forced into
unnatural pronunciation for comic purposes in
order to make a rhyme.

(*gulf, her / sulphur*)   (*dwelling / colonelling*)
(*ecclesiastic / a stick*)

Multiple rhyme – consists of 3 or more
syllables.

>   (*feasible / please able*)
>   (*listlessness / witlessness*)

Monorhyme – is a long string of lines that
rhyme with the same sound

>   *…..so*

>   *…..know*

>   *…..slow*

..... *snow*

Onomatopoeia – imitation of actual sounds.

(*moaning* doves / *murmuring* bees)

Pitch is what we hear when we refer to a voice being high or low.

Pitch   **H - L** (Occurs in recitals of lists usually)

    L - H   (Gives the impression that the speaker still has something to say)

    L - L   (Declarative Sentences)

    H - H   (Yes/No question)

Boundaries between prosodic phrases

-Is when the speaker sometime slows down

-Might be an abrupt change in the pitch

-The last syllable of each prosodic phrase is typically quite long

Stress may be indicated by a mixture of raised intonation, lengthening of word, and raised intensity.

    (I only took **TWO** biscuits.)
    (I only took two **BISCUITS**)

Tone of voice is the way your voice sounds. My voice can sound *mad*, *happy*, *excited*, *scared*, *sad*, and *regular*.

Find rhymes by adding new beginnings to word ends thinking of every letter in the alphabet.

Slant rhyme is word that almost sound alike.

Alliteration (same beginning sounds)
    Ex.   _S_aying _S_oon I'm....

Assonance (same vowel sounds)
    Ex.   And we went to Theed to see the queen.

Consonance (Same consonant sounds)
    Ex. The coun_c_il wa_s_ impre_ss_ed, of cour_s_e.

When you want the feel of a line to be slow and dreamy use multiple syllable words. If you want the line to be read quickly use short words with hard consonant sounds such as T and K.

Chapter 4

LYRIC WRITING

In this chapter we dive deeper into your world as a great writer. If you have studied chapters 1-3 up to this point. You should already be well on your way to be coming the MC you want to be. Chapter four will teach you the technical part of lyric writing. A lot of the technical aspects are probably stuff you already do. But its good to put a name on it. So you have structure. Lets take a look shall we.

Much of lyric writing is technical

(**rhyme, rhythm, contrast, balance,** and **repetition**)

Object writing is when you pick a real object and focus on it. The more senses you incorporate into your writing the better it breaths and dances.

-**Organis sense** – inner body functions (*heartbeat, pulse, cramps*   etc.)

-**Kinesthetic sense** – roughly your sense of the world around you (when you get drunk or sea sick the world around you blurs like blurred vision)

7 Senses (**sight, hearing, smell, taste, touch, organic, kinesthetic**)

Metaphors are the mainstay of good lyric writing

3 Types

-Expressed Identity – asserts identity between 2 nouns

    (*fear is a shadow*)

3 Forms of expressed identity

    -x is y (*fear is a shadow*)

    -the y of x (*the shadow of fear*)

    -x's y (*fear's shadow*)

-can even extend them to longer versions
(*clouds are sailing ships / on rivers of wind*)

-Qualifying Metaphors – Adjective qualify nouns, Adverbs qualify Verbs. Friction within these relationships create metaphor.

    (*Hasty clouds / to sing blindly*)

-Verbal Metaphor – formed by conflict between the verb and its subject/and or object.

(*clouds sail / he tortured his clutch / frost gobbles summer down*)

Dratonic Relationship – words grouped together in close relationship.

    (Power; Avalanche; Mahammad Ali; Army etc.)

A good way to find metaphors is to ask these 2 questions.

-What characteristics does my idea have?

-What else has those characteristics?

Adjectives + Nouns- you can make vivid adj out of verbs.

Ex. to wrinkle becomes the adjective wrinkled, wrinkled water or wrinkling (the wrinkling hours). **These are called participles.**

Nouns + Verbs- (these are harder to do because we are used to looking at things in the world rather than actions.

Verbs + Nouns

Nouns + Adjectives

Adverbs + Verbs also Verbs + Adverbs

Expressive Objects or situations are called "objective correlatives" – objects anyone can *touch*, *smell*, or *see* that correlate with the emotion you want to express.

When you stimulate your listeners senses they pick pictures from their own personal sense files.

Each family in Family rhymes(below) sound exactly alike. Meaning all voiced plosive sound the same. For example bag would sound exactly like cab and had. B,D,and G are all in the same family. The voiced plosives family. These word endings incorporated within your rhymes can do wonders. Keep this in mind when you write your lyrics.

Family Rhyme

	Plosives	Fricatives	Nasals
voiced	b d g	v th z zh j	m n ng
unvoiced	p t k	f th s sh ch	

Nuclear Syllable usually appears at the end of a intonation group.

-Linda was wearing that black **skirt**
(Normal placement)

-Linda was wearing that **black** skirt
(Not a red one)

-Linda was wearing **that** black skirt
(Particular skirt already referred to)

-Linda was **wearing** that black skirt
(Not just carrying it)

(**unmarked tonic stress, emphatic stress, contrastive stress, new info stress**)

> -stress applies to individual syllables and most commonly involves (**loudness, length**) and (**higher, pitch**) The Official Hip-Hop Manual shows loudness in our rhymes with CAPITAL LETTERS. Pitch is shown either high pitch or low pitch. High pitch is shown with a parenthesis over the word (sort of like a mountain covering the word) and low pitch is show with a parenthesis under the word.

Basic rule of songwriting is **keep your listeners interested from beginning to end.**

Versus get us ready to hear the chorus like parts of an essay each one should focus on a separate idea. They say the chorus makes a song. But I believe if you combine hot versus with hot choruses you have a classic. Don't you agree?

There will always be 3 perspectives when ever you tell a story no matter what.

3 perspectives

-I (me)

-You

-We

Opening and closing lines of any lyric section are naturally strong. If you want people to notice an important idea put it in a **power position.** Whenever creating a special effect with your structure you call attention to what you are saying. This extra focus gives the position its power.

Power Positions are opening/closing positions, and surprises like shorter, longer, or extra lines.

Verses should relate. Lyrics accumulate power when verses work together.

Verbs determine verses. (past, present, future)

Controlling verbs is the key to controlling tenses.

-Using the **ing** form of the verb (*losing*) Omit any helping verbs (*losing* instead of *is losing*, *was losing*, *will be losing*) Don't mistake the **ing** form for verbal adjectives participles (a losing strategy) or for verbal nouns (gerunds) eg. (losing builds character)

   -Use the form of the verb infinitive and omit the main verb (to   lose rather than I hate to lose)

   -Omit verbs altogether

Pronouns determine point of view.

3rd person narrative acts as a story teller directing the audience to an objective world.

3rd person	Singular	Plural
Subject	he she it	they
Direct Object	him her it	them
Positive Adj.	his her its	their
Pos. Predicate	his hers its	theirs
Positive Adjective	"That is *her*......."	
Positive Predicate	"The........is *hers*."	

2nd person	Singular	Plural
Subject	you	you
Direct Object	you	you
Poss Adjective	your	your
Poss Predicate	yours	yours

1st person also story telling

	Singular	Plural
Subject	I	we
Direct Object	me	us
Positive Adj.	my	our
Pos. Predicate	mine	ours

Don't give the facts to someone who already knows them like **(you)**

1st person tells about a conversation he/she actually had with a 3rd party

    (**He asked me** what a gifts can I bring…..)

Direct Address – person is talking directly to us or unseen you.

    (**I asked you** "what gifts can I bring…..)

3rd Person – is a story teller pointing to a scene

    (**He asked her** "what gifts can I bring")

Content / Stressed words			Function / Unstressed words	
Verbs	Question words	Modal	Auxiliaries	Pronoun
Nouns	Prepositional Adv.		Articles	
Adj.	Negatives		Conjunctions	
Adverbs			Prepositions	

Emphatic Stress is moved to content words to express emphasis on that word.

```
It was very Boring  (unmarked)
You mustn't talk so LOUDly    (unmarked)
```

```
     It was VEry boring  (emphatic)You MUSTN'T
talk so loudly (emphatic)
```

Some **intensifying adverbs** and **modifiers** (or their derivatives) are **emphatic** by nature.

```
    (Indeed, utterly, terrific, tremendous)
```

Contrastive Stress is a contractible stressed word.

```
    Do you like this one or THAT one?  I like
    THIS one
```

Chapter 5

TONE & PITCH

In this chapter we will focus on tone and pitch. This is important because the tone and pitch of our voice plays a big roll in communication when speaking. You can tell a lot about how a person feels from the pitch or tone of their voice. For example as a kid I remember I could tell by the tone of my moms voice if she was happy , mad or sad when she spoke. So be sure to pay attention when you speak and incorporate this in your rhymes.

Nuclear Syllable sounds louder than other stressed syllables and also has change of pitch.

  -Two most common are (rising / falling pitch) also possible to have (fall-rising / rise-falling pitch)

  -Fall Rising   ex. When would it suit you to come home? Now? (expresses a question would it be ok. If I came now)

  -Rise Falling   ex. When would it suit you to come home? Now (expresses a statement I'll come now)

  -Rising   ex. There coming on Monday / aren't they. (statement anticipating listeners agreement)

  -Falling ex. There coming on Monday / aren't they? (Question seeking an answer yes or no)

Falling Tone shows completeness and normally used when a person is about to stop talking.

Falling Tone at the end of a list shows list is complete.

    Ex. Would you like tea, coffee, fruit juice, or *lemonade*? (that's all I'm offering)

Rising Tone shows incompleteness, if tone ends in rising tone the person wishes to continue speaking and seeking feed back by word or gesture.

Rising Tone shows there are other drinks.

Ex. Would you like tea, coffee, fruit juice, *lemonade*... (there might be other drinks as well that haven't been mentioned)

Pitch change indicates certainty, uncertainty, enthusiasm, boredom etc.

Prosody features describe **pitch, loudness, tempo,** and **rhythm**

Loudness is associated with anger (can also be indicated by very quiet, tense speech)

    -Can also relate to strong weak syllables and in the extra prominence given to nuclear syllables

    -**Very loud and quiet utters** help arouse strong emotion in audiences

    -**Tempo** is pace of speech and can be varied

    -**Fast Speech** show emergency

    -**Slow Speech** is used for emphasis

    -**Varying tempo along with changes in**
    -**loudness** is also used in public speaking

Paralinguistic features are vocal effects employed when speaking and referred to as tone of voice and can make our speech breathy, nasal, husky, or creaky, lip rounding, low breathy voice.

Ex. (**Whispering, Giggling** and **laughing**)

Phoraesthetic words associated with certain meanings

Sl(*slippery / slimy / sluggish*)
Sh(*crash / smash / crush*)
K(*crack / whack / flick*)

Elision (lost sounds) is in rapid speech when some sounds are left out and often occurs with clusters of constants.

(Postman / pos(**t**)man)

(Mashed potatoes / Mash(**ed**) Potatoes)

-Some words are hard to pronounce with out elision

(*Asthma / facts / twelfths*)

-Weak vowels also get elided

(library / lib(**ra**)ry)
(Policeman / P(**o**)liceman)

Rhythm can be heard when counting aloud

(*Five / ten / fifteen / twenty*) Stressed syllables are lengthened in <u>*five*</u> and <u>*ten*</u>, and shortened in <u>*fifteen*</u> and <u>*twenty*</u> so words with two syllables are the same length.

Rhythm speech is produced through combining stressed and unstressed syllables.

-Nursery rhymes sound rhetorical

> *This* is the / *house* that / *Jack* / *built*
> *Humpty* / *Dumpty* / *sat* on a / *wall*

Pitch Movement - variations in pitch = voice going up and down (not singing) pitch movement effects a single word. You can convey different meaning by changing pitch of a word.

Tone groups are said on a single breath (limited in length). They average about 2 seconds or about five words.

Spoken language is broken into **tone groups** because we need to breath, and tend to carry one idea at a time. Its necessary to pause and draw breath, these *planned pauses* are called voice hesitations and often marked by um or er.

When passage is delivered at fast tempo / tone groups are an average longer than other speech.

Division of a sentence in a tone group can affect the meaning in some cases.

Do you take sugar? I don't / no (Idon't, no)

I don't know / (I don't know)

Intonation should include 4 major features (**Intonation units, Tones, Stress, Pitch Range**)

 -Every intonation unit has a type of tonic stress

-Tones - **fall** / **low-rise** / **high-rise** / **fall-rise** - these tones are assigned to the voice movement on the tonic syllable

-All units have **3 pitch levels** (keys) **High - Mid - Low**

Pausing is a way of packaging info. , also notifies change of meaning. Certain pauses in a stream of speech can have significant meaning variations in the message.

(*Those who sold quickly / made a profit*)
A profit is made those who sold quickly

(*Those who sold / quickly made a profit*)
A profit was quickly made by those who sold

Part II

4 TYPES OF TONE

Direction of the pitch movement on the last stressed syllable is what makes a tone falling or rising.

If the **tonic syllable** is in its final position the glide continues over the rest of the syllables.

A fall in pitch on the tonic syllable redeems the tone as fall. A rise tone is when the tonic syllable is the start of a upward glide of pitch.

2 kinds of glide:-If upward movement is higher then it's a high - rise

-If lower then it's a low - rise

Fall rise - has first a pitch fall and then rise.

Fall is a falling tone

-A **falling tone** is what is most commonly used. Signals a sense of finality, completion, and belief in the content of the utterance etc.

(I'll rep*ort* you to the **HEAD** master)

-A **falling tone** may be used in referring expressions as well.

(I've *spo*ken with the **CLEA**ner)

-**Questions** that begin with (**wh**) are generally pronounced with a falling tone.

(Where is the **PEN**cil?)

-**Imperative statements** have a **falling tone.**

(Go and see a **DOC**tor) (T*ake* a **SEAT**)

-**Request or orders**

(P*lease* sit **DOWN**) (Call him **IN**)

-**Exclamations**

(W*atch* **OUT**)

-**Yes / No** questions seeking or expecting confirmation and the response to it may be lengthened.

(You *like* it **DON'T** you?) (**YEES**)

-**Yes / No** question if speaker uses a falling tone we assume he already knows the answer.

(H*ave* you **MET** him) (**YES**)

Low Rise (A rising Tone)

-**Yes / No** question where the speaker does not
know the answer and the addressee knows the
answer.

>   (I*sn't* he **NICE**) (Yes, **NO**, I don't know)

>   -Other examples of a rising tone

>   (Do you *want* some **COF**fee)
>   (Do you take **CREAM** in your coffee)

High Rise (A rising Tone)

-If tonic stress is uttered with extra pitch
height, we think the speaker is asking for
repetition, clarification or indicating
disbelief.

>   (I'm *taking* up **TA**xidermy this <u>au</u>tumn)
>   (*Ta*king up **WHAT**?) - Clarification
>   (She *passed* her **DRI**ving *test*)
>   (She **PASSED**) - Disbelief

-The 3 tones above can be used in independent,
single intonation units.

Fall Rise (followed by fall)

-Generally used in dependent intonation units
like those involving sentential adverbs,
subordinate clauses, compound sentences and so
on.

-Signals dependency, continuity, and non -
finality.

-Examples (slash indicates pause)

>   (*Pri*vate enter**PRISE** / is always **EF**ficient)
>   (A *quick* tour of the **CI**ty / would be **NICE**)
>   (Pre**SU**mably / he *thinks* he **CAN**)
>   (*U*sually / he *comes* on SUNDAY)

Fall Rise + Fall

-Most complex clause types is one that has dependent (adverbial or subordinate) clause followed by and independent (main) clause. Such a clause has two intonation units. The first, non-final normally has a fall-rise. The second, final has a fall tone.

> (*When* I *passed* my **REA**ding *test* / I was **VE**ry happy)

> (If you **SEE** him / *give* my **MES**sage)

Fall + Fall Rise

-When the order of complex clause is reversed we still observe the pattern fall-rise and fall respectively.

> (I **WON'T** deliver the *goods* / *un*less I rec*eive* the **PAY**ment)

> (The m*oon* rev*ol*ves around the **EARTH** /as we **ALL** know)

> (*Private* enter*prise* is always **EF**ficient / where as *public* ownership means Inefficient.)

-Final intonation units have a falling tone and non - final ones have a fall-rise.

> (He joined the **AR**my / and *spent* all his *time* in **AL**dershot)

> (My *sister* who is a **NURSE** / has **ONE** child)

-Some of these tones can be used when a sentence has more than one intonation unit.

Fall Rise + Low Rise

-This tone pattern involves a dependent clause followed by a yes/no question

    (If I **HELPED** you / would you *try* a**GAIN**?)

    (De*spite* its **DRAW**backs / do you *favor* it or **NOT**?)

Fall + Fall

-We the speaker demands agreement as in tag questions

    (It's a bit **TOO** good to be *true* / **ISN'T** it?)

-Reinforcing adverbials can have a fall when place utterance finality has an expression of after thought.

    (*Ann* said she'd *help* as *much* as she **COULD** / **NATU**rally)

-If two actions are part of a sequence

    (She's *28* years **OLD** / and *lives* in **GIPPS**land)

Pitch and Pitch Range (key)

-**Loudness** contributes to the make up of pitch.

-**Higher pitch** is heard louder than lower pitch.

-**Syllable length** contributes to final tonic stress more than pitch.

-**The 3 keys are High, Mid, Low**

    -**Speaker** must choose **1 of 3 keys** required for conversation

-**Most speech** is at the **mid** (unmarked) key in normal/unemotional speech

-**High/Low key** is marked:

-**High key** - is used for emotionally charged intonation units.

-**Low key** - indicates an existence of equivalence (as in appositive expressions) and less significant t the speech.

-**Syllabic Pitch** is always higher than the utterance pitch. In some sense syllabic pitch is one step ahead of the utterance pitch.

High Key

-Exclamation refers to actions described by verbs such as cry, scream, shout, wait and shriek are all usually done with high pitch.

(Oh **GOD**!)

-The act of Echo/Repeating is almost always done with a high pitch.

Low Key

-Indicated wit Co-reference and Appositions.

-The word away in Low Key is co-referential with you in mid key

High

Mid / I **TOLD** you *already* /

Low   DUMmy /

-Non defining relative clauses, parenthetical statements expressions of dis - agreement, etc.

High

Mid / My **DOC**tor /   /is very **WELL** known

Low   *whos* a neu**ROI**logist

-Statements of opinion

5 main sentence clauses

1. Statement, answer, ? Request, exclamation

2. Familiarity, unfamiliarity

3. Emphatic, unemphatic

4. Contrastive, non-contrastive

5. Expressiveness, inexpressiveness

1. **Falling**   (Statements, Exclamations)

2. **Rising** (Non-Final, Questions)

3. **Level**   (Progredience, Incompleteness)

4. **Falling - Rising** (uncertainty)

5. **Rising - Falling** (certainty, obviousness)

Chapter 6

MUSIC

In chapter 6 we are getting closer and closer to our knowledge and understanding of your craft. Now we'll take you through the basics of music. Pay close attention and you might learn something. (Laugh) Okay lets begin.

Learn to think in common meter and cram your ideas into alternating four stress and three stress phrases. If they resist see what surprises might come about.

Common meter organizes music into a single eight bar unit

(2 bars and 2 bars) + (2 bars and 2 bars)

-The second line of common meter, bars 3 and 4, contains only three stresses. Keeping the entire system moving until it is matched at line 4 (bars 7 and 8)

-When you want to rap in 4 bar units instead of 8 match bars 1 and 2 with 3 and 4

Couplets rhyme marking a stopping place for the ear. They form a lyrical and musical unit of four bars long. They move us forward with 4 stressed notes in each 2 bar section.

♪ ♪ ♪ ♪ / ♪ ♪ ♪ ♪

You can easily extend from 4 to 6 lines
without getting to far off balance.

In chapter 7 **The Official How To Rap
Manual** shows bars and measurements as
circles or dots. We call these points.
In other words each bar has eight points.
Each point is open or closed, closed
meaning solid. You will be taken further
on this idea in chapter 7.

Prosody lining up words and notes,
matching stressed notes with stressed
syllables, could create a relationship
between rhythm and meaning by writing
about a galloping horse in a clippity -
clap rhythm, could also use strings of
stressed syllables to slow the rhythm
down.

You know what you want to say so you
have to design form to support your
ideas. Tools for designing your lyrics
shapes, lengths, rhythms and rhyme
schemes. For example you might try
putting rhymes (both phrase- end and
internal rhyme) close together and try
using short phrases.

A even number of phrases creates a
balanced section and an odd number
creates an unbalanced section.

-Unbalanced sections make you want to
move to find a stable spot.

-Balanced sections stop motion.

Balancing / Unbalancing a lyric in the right place gives you 4 audience grabbing strategies.

-Spot lighting important ideas.

-Pushing one section forward into another section.

-Contrastingly one section with another one.

-Setting up a need for balancing a section or phrase.

Always take time on your trigger lines.

Chapter 7

BARS AND COUNTS

Okay now we are going to dive into one of the most important chapters of this book, bars and counts. I gave you a brief description of this in chapter 6. Now lets look deeper into this. I may be the only person who writes like this or it is possible I may not be. But I remember when writing my rhymes I would put a dot(point) over the word so I know exactly how I wanted to say it over the beat. Just like the examples of the verses at the end of chapter 2. Not only that but that point let me know where I was at and how far I had to go to complete a 16 bar verse.

I knew with the technique I invented if I counted 32 points I had 16 bars. (16x2) Each bar has 2 main points. Before I lose you let me explain further. I came up with 8 counts, or you can say 8 points within each bar. We have 4 solid points(The points in the example verses are 2 out of the main 4 which are the solids) and 4 not solid points. The 4 solid points are solid because they land on the primary position in a unit of measure or bar. This primary position is basically where the beat falls. For example tap your finger on the table now, right now 4 times. Okay good now do that four more times keeping the same rhythm. 1,2,3,4,1,2,3,4.........or 1,2,3,4,5,6,7,8.

Now be sure to count out load or in your head with each tap. Now you know 8 points that's 1bar. Do that 16 times and that's the length of 1 verse. Now do that same thing over again. Now this time on 1 start with your fist and 2 with your fingernail, but only do it in a 4 count measure, meaning only count to 4. So it's like this-fist, nail, fist, nail, a count of 4. Now **The Official How To Rap Manual** shows this as fists and nails being solid points and the space that is between fist and nails(of course when your not tapping) are not solid points. Try this a few times tapping with a bit and you should get the picture. Get this down now because you will be putting words together within these points.

Now lets take this 1 step further. All solid and not solid points are equal. Meaning you can start your rhyme anywhere within that 8 count and anywhere within that 4 count. For example 1 bar can be started and ended on all 4 solids and then also fit within all 4 not solids. Get it? Hope so.

Now lets look at this 8 count a little farther. **The Official How To Rap Manual** shows this 8 count like O●O●O●O●. The 4th and 8th count will always have a line directly in the center of them. The first line shows a half a bar(the first 4 points) and the second line completes a full bar(the 8th point). So it looks like this:

Note between every point there is a ½ point. Big would utilize this a lot in his rhymes. The solid points are the

primary position.   The two points with
the lines in them are usually where the
treble hits within a song landing on
points 4 and 8.

Now below, remember how I told you
all points are equal? So notice under
the heading 8 count I have 2 bars to show
comparison. On each side of the 2 bars I
have 2 group of numbers. The left side
shows the original. The right side in
parenthesis is its equal. For example 1-
8 count is equal to 5-4 count. In other
words a rhyme starting in 1 and ending on
8 counts is equal to a rhyme starting at
5 and ending on a 4 count. Get it? Now I
break this down all the way to a 2 count.
1 count is just that one point over each
count. Thats sort of self explanatory.
One syllable usually fits on one point.
A quick Two syllable word can also fit on
one point. An extremely fast three
syllable word is possible but Twister
will have to spit that for you.(Laugh) So
now that you studied the verse examples
try rhyming within each of these points
from 1-8 or 2-6. Shouldn't be hard. But
if you have questions contact me. I will
write you back. Okay now get to it.

8 Counts   ○●○◐○●○◑   Between every point there is a ½ point

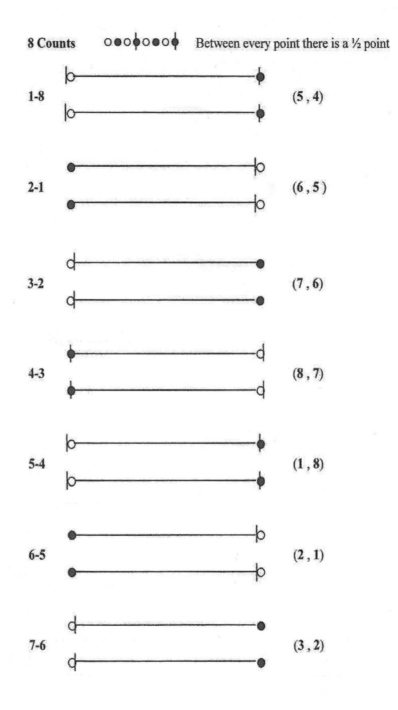

1-8   (5 , 4)

2-1   (6 , 5)

3-2   (7 , 6)

4-3   (8 , 7)

5-4   (1 , 8)

6-5   (2 , 1)

7-6   (3 , 2)

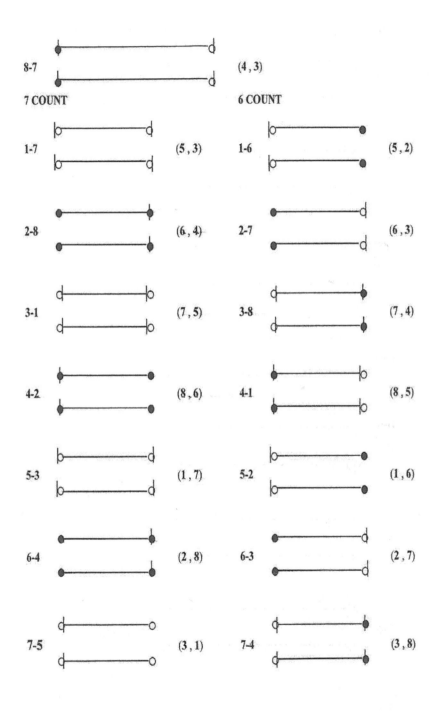

8-7   (4 , 3)

7 COUNT   6 COUNT

1-7   (5 , 3)   1-6   (5 , 2)

2-8   (6 , 4)   2-7   (6 , 3)

3-1   (7 , 5)   3-8   (7 , 4)

4-2   (8 , 6)   4-1   (8 , 5)

5-3   (1 , 7)   5-2   (1 , 6)

6-4   (2 , 8)   6-3   (2 , 7)

7-5   (3 , 1)   7-4   (3 , 8)

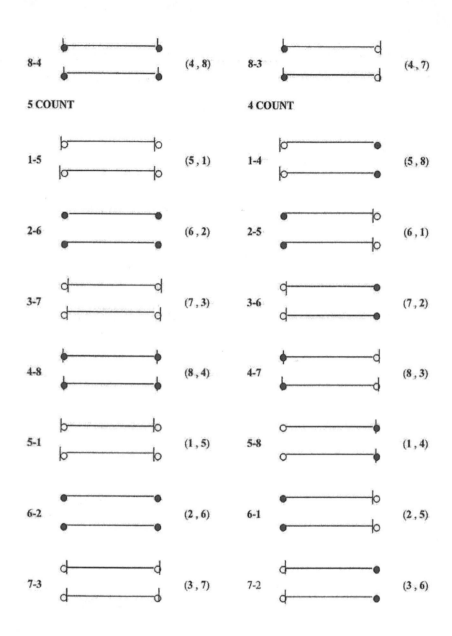

8-4 (4, 8) 8-3 (4, 7)

5 COUNT **4 COUNT**

1-5 (5, 1) 1-4 (5, 8)

2-6 (6, 2) 2-5 (6, 1)

3-7 (7, 3) 3-6 (7, 2)

4-8 (8, 4) 4-7 (8, 3)

5-1 (1, 5) 5-8 (1, 4)

6-2 (2, 6) 6-1 (2, 5)

7-3 (3, 7) 7-2 (3, 6)

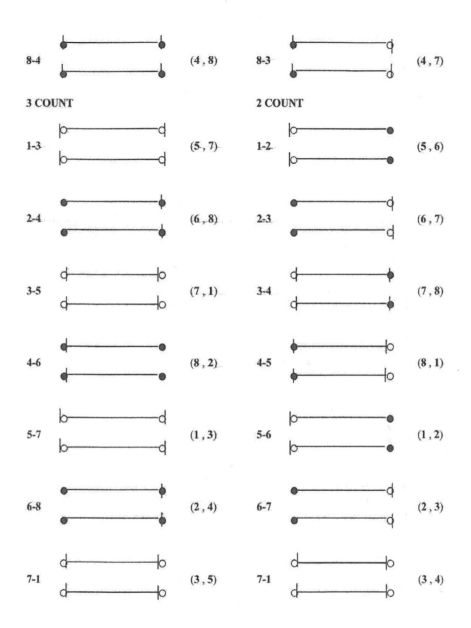

8-4 (4 , 8)   8-3 (4 , 7)

3 COUNT   **2 COUNT**

1-3 (5 , 7)   1-2 (5 , 6)

2-4 (6 , 8)   2-3 (6 , 7)

3-5 (7 , 1)   3-4 (7 , 8)

4-6 (8 , 2)   4-5 (8 , 1)

5-7 (1 , 3)   5-6 (1 , 2)

6-8 (2 , 4)   6-7 (2 , 3)

7-1 (3 , 5)   7-1 (3 , 4)

Now below practice combinations of different
bars. In other words try rhyming a 1-6 count
bar with a 1-8 count bar. I have a whole list
of combos below.

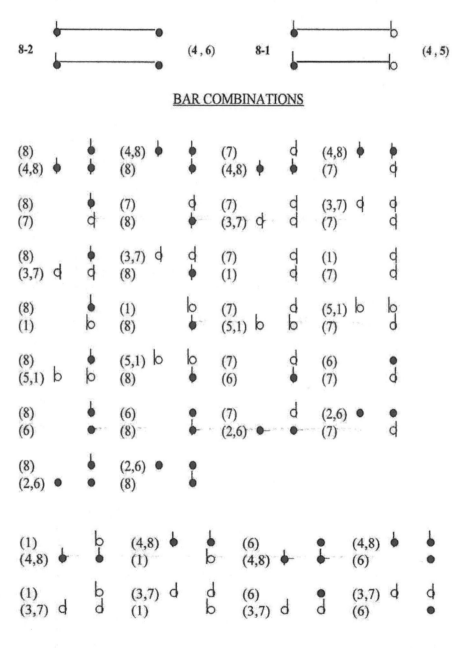

BAR COMBINATIONS

(1)   (5,1)   (6)   (5,1)
(5,1)   (1)   (5,1)   (6)

(1)   (6)   (6)   (2,6)
(6)   (1)   (2,6)   (6)

(1)   (2,6)
(2,6)   (1)

(4,8)   (3,7)   (4,7)
(3,7)   (4,8)   (4,1)
                                      (4,6)
(4,8)   (5,1)   (3,8)
(5,1)   (4,8)   (3,1)
                                        (3,6)
(4,8)   (2,6)   (5,8)
(2,6)   (4,8)   (5,7)
                                        (5,6)
(3,7)   (5,1)   (2,8)
(5,1)   (3,7)   (2,7)
                                        (2,1)
(3,7)   (2,6)
(2,6)   (3,7)

(5,1)   (2,6)
(2,6)   (5,1)

1-8   2-1   3-2   8-7
1-7   2-8   3-1   8-6
1-6   2-7   3-8   8-5
1-5   2-6   3-7   8-4
1-4   2-5   3-6   8-3
1-3   2-4   3-5   8-2
1-2   2-3   3-4   8-1

1-8   1-7   1-6   1-5
2-8   2-7   2-6   2-5
3-8   3-7   3-6   3-5
8-4   8-3   8-2   8-1

73

1	2	3	4	1	2	3	4	
LINES 1-8	2-1	3-2	8-7	5-4	6-5	7-6	4-3	Shows how you can
1-7	2-8	3-1	8-6	5-3	6-4	7-5	4-2	combine certain lines
1-6	2-7	3-8	8-5	5-2	6-3	7-4	4-1	together to make your
1-5	2-6	3-7	8-4	5-1	6-2	7-3	4-8	verses.
1-4	2-5	3-6	8-3	5-8	6-1	7-2	4-7	
1-3	2-4	3-5	8-2	5-7	6-8	7-1	4-6	
1-2	2-3	3-4	8-1	5-6	6-7	7-8	4-5	

Points 1 2 3 4 5 6 7 8 1 Shows how different points can make different
2 3 4 5 6 7 8 1 2 lines.
3 4 5 6 7 8 1 2 3
4 5 6 7 8 1 2 3 4
5 6 7 8 1 2 3 4 5
6 7 8 1 2 3 4 5 6
7 8 1 2 3 4 5 6 7
8 1 2 3 4 5 6 7 8

Rhyme can be started and ended at any point

—Half a point before or after all points

—One full point before or after any point

—Or exactly on any 1 point

    —Also 3 or 4 points before or after all points (Below is equivalent to a 16 bar verse)

Rhyme 4 ← Primary(Before) 1- 4 /→ Secondary 5-8 (After) Shows Rhyme points and patterns

O	●	O	●	O	●	O	●
1	2	3	4	5	6	7	8
2	3	4	5	6	7	8	9
3	4	5	6	7	8	9	10
4	5	6	7	8	9	10	11
5	6	7	8	9	10	11	12
6	7	8	9	10	11	12	13
7	8	9	10	11	12	13	14
8	9	10	11	12	13	14	15
9	10	11	12	13	14	15	16

```
10   11   12   13   14   15   16    1
11   12   13   14   15   16    1    2
12   13   14   15   16    1    2    3
13   14   15   16    1    2    3    4
14   15   16    1    2    3    4    5
15   16    1    2    3    4    5    6
16    1    2    3    4    5    6    7
```

Below shows where words rhyme. For example lets
look at 1 word rhyme L1. Under that we have the
number 1 followed by other numbers in
parenthesis. This shows how you can make one
word or one syllable words rhyme within a line.
So lets say you make point 1, which is the 1
followed by parenthesis under the 1 word rhyme
section, rhyme within that line with a word in
point 8. So it would be similar to bar one
looking like "Plush all I do is make the ladies
fuss". Get it? Plush lands on point 1 and
fuss on point 8. You can do the same with 2
word or 2 syllable words as well. Even with 3
syllable words. Its all right there for you to
try. Lets try one more with 2 word rhyme. This
time we will use **34**and**78**. Thats a easy one. "I
move to quick in my drop blue whip" Points 3
and 4 is to quick while 7 and 8 is blue whip.
Now you try a few.

Line 1

1 Word Rhyme L1	2 Word	L1	3 Word	L1
1 (8,7,6,5,4,3,2)	12(34, 45, 56, 67,78)	123 (456, 567, 678)		
2 (8,7,6,5,4,3)	23(45, 56, 67,78, 81)	234 (567, 678)		
3 (8,7,6,5,4)	34 (56, 67, 78, 81)	345 (678)		
4 (8,7,6,5)	45 (67, 78, 81)	678		
5 (8,7,6)	56 (78, 81)			
6 (8,7)	67 (81)			
7 (8)				

Line 2

L2 1 Word

8 (16, 15, 14, 13, 12, 11, 10)
7 (16, 15, 14, 13, 12, 11, 10, 9)
6 (16, 15, 14, 13, 12, 11, 10, 9, 8)
5 (16, 15, 14, 13, 12, 11, 10, 9, 8, 7)
4 (16, 15, 14, 13, 12, 11, 10, 9, 8, 7, 6)
3 (16, 15, 14, 13, 12, 11, 10, 9, 8, 7, 6, 5)
2 (16, 15, 14, 13, 12, 11, 10, 9, 8, 7, 6, 5, 4)
1 (16, 15, 14, 13, 12, 11, 10, 9, 8, 7, 6, 5, 4, 3)

L2 2 Word

12 (34, 45, 56, 67, 78, 89, 910, 1011, 1112, 1213, 1314, 1415, 1516)
23 (45, 56, 67, 78, 89, 910, 1011, 1112, 1213, 1314, 1415, 1516, 161)
34 (56, 67, 78, 89, 910, 1011, 1112, 1213, 1314, 1415, 1516, 161, 12)
45 (67, 78, 89, 910, 1011, 1112, 1213, 1314, 1415, 1516, 161, 12, 23)
56 (78, 89, 910, 1011, 1112, 1213, 1314, 1415, 1516, 161, 12, 23, 34)
67 (89, 910, 1011, 1112, 1213, 1314, 1415, 1516, 161, 12, 23, 34, 45)
78 (910, 1011, 1112, 1213, 1314, 1415, 1516, 161, 12, 23, 34, 45, 56)
89 (1011, 1112, 1213, 1314, 1415, 1516, 161, 12, 23, 34, 45, 56, 67)

L2 3 Word

123 (456, 567, 678, 789, 8910, 91011, 101112, 111213, 121314, 131415, 141516)
234 (567, 678, 789, 8910, 91011, 101112, 111213, 121314, 131415, 141516, 15161)
345 (678, 789, 8910, 91011, 101112, 111213, 121314, 131415, 141516, 15161, 1612)
456 (789, 8910, 91011, 101112, 111213, 121314, 131415, 141516, 15161, 1612, 123)

4 WAYS LINES BEGIN

```
8  1  2  3  4  5  6  7              2  3  4  5  6  7  8  1
●  ○  ●  ○  ◑  ○  ●  ○              ●  ○  ◑  ○  ●  ○  ◑  ○
1  2  3  4  5  6  7  8              3  4  5  6  7  8  1  2
○  ●  ○  ◑  ○  ●  ○  ◑              ○  ◑  ○  ●  ○  ◑  ○  ●
```

1 SYLLABLE   **2 SYLLABLE**   **3 SYLLABLE**
CHILL   MONEY   MEDICINE

2 1 SYLLABLE WORDS together can replace 2 SYLLABLE POINTS

Ex. Take That

-Even think about making the consonant sounds match and stand out putting that extra emphasis on the beginnings and endings. Also focus on consonants said in frontal lip area.

-Also make words rhyme with similar syllable structure.

| J **spit it** | bang**sy** | **ex**pose |
| they **did it** | Made **me** | **up** those |

Chapter 8

Combination Syllables

* For 3 and 2 word Syllables they can be said quick or regular. Slow is regular. A quick 2 syllable word is similar to Pac example verse at the end of chapter 2 at bars 13 and 14 and the words struggle and trouble. These are 2 syllable quick words. You can also use 1 syllable quick words as well though they are not shown here. Now the singy syllables are similar to Pac and Big's flow. "Crack Feeeen Momma". Play around with them a little bit to make them a little longer or a little shorter. They usually have to cover 2 points to be considered singy but they can carry more than that. I incorporated this a few times in my rhymes and I thought it sounded pretty good. As a reminder, the underline under a a syllable shows where length of the syllable is stressed.

<u>1Syllable words: Slow</u>
1a flow
1b Ben/zo
1c Move/pass/hoes
1d Cant/kids/move/me
1f Tha-streets

<u>2 Syllable words: Quick</u>
2a Gotta
2b Gotta/dolla
2c popa/little/henney
2d if he/knew da/way the/spit it

<u>3 Syllable words:</u> Quick
3a memory
3b benefit/cinnomon
3c memory/benefit/cinnamon

<u>Combinations</u>
1a + 2a Calf Muscle
1a + 3a its dem again

2a + 1a poppa shit
2a + 3a Sippen Hennesy

Singy Syllables

1a flow	2a gotta	3a Memory
1b ben/zo	2b gotta dolla	3b benefit/cinnamon
1c Move Pass Hoes	2c poppa little henney	3c memory/benefit/cinnamon
1d Cant Kids Move Me	2d ifhe knewda wayshe spitit	
1e Get That dough quick fast		
1f Tha-streets		

* All 2's and 3's are sung on last syllable .

You can also sing on the last consonant
(Freshshshshshsh)

This is the last and final chapter. Study
this book as much as possible. Let me know what
you come up with. I would like to hear the
greats. Please continue to send in any
suggestions about this book that you may have to
Staff@how2rap.com. And support your local artists
as well. We need to be more creative in this
game. And I hope you've learned something from
my trials and tribulations as an artist. Good
luck. One

Jamaal "J-Mill" West

Practice

Tables

Suffix	Example	Suffix	Example
ed	walk + ed = walked	ness	happy + ness = happiness
ing	say + ing = saying	al	accident + al = accidental
er	tall + er = taller	ary	imagine + ary = imaginary
tion	educate + tion = education	able	accept + able = acceptable
sion	divide + sion = division	ly	love + ly = lovely
cian	music + cian = musician	ment	excite + ment = excitement
fully	hope + fully = hopefully	ful	help + ful + helpful
est	large + est = largest	y	ease + y = easy

General Roots and Prefixes

Root or Prefix	Meaning	Examples
a, an	not, without	atheist, anarchy, anonymous apathy, aphasia, anemia
ab	away from	absent, abduction, aberrant, abstemious
ambul	to walk	ambulatory, amble, ambulance, somnambulist
ante	before	anteroom, antebellum, antedate antecedent, antediluvian
anti, ant	against, opposite	antisocial, antiseptic, antithesis, antibody, antichrist, antinomies, antifreeze, antipathy, antigen, antibiotic
audi	to hear	audience, auditory, audible, auditorium, audiovisual, audition
be	thoroughly	bedecked, besmirch, besprinkled
auto	self	automobile, automatic, autograph, autonomous, autoimmune
bene	good, well	benefactor, beneficial, benevolent, benediction, beneficiary, benefit
cede, ceed, cess	to go, to yield	succeed, proceed, precede, recede, secession, exceed, succession

chron	time	chronology, chronic, chronicle chronometer, anachronism
cide, cis	to kill, to cut	fratricide, suicide, incision, excision, circumcision
circum	around	circumnavigate, circumflex, circumstance, circumcision, circumference, circumorbital, circumlocution, circumvent, circumscribe, circulatory
clud, clus claus	to close	include, exclude, clause, claustrophobia, enclose, exclusive, reclusive, conclude
con, com	with, together	convene, compress, contemporary, converge, compact, confluence, concatenate, conjoin, combine
contra, counter	against, opposite	contradict, counteract, contravene, contrary, counterspy, contrapuntal
cred	to believe	credo, credible, credence, credit, credential, credulity, incredulous
cycl	circle, wheel	bicycle, cyclical, cycle, encliclical
de	from, down, away	detach, deploy, derange, deodorize, devoid, deflate, degenerate, deice
dei, div	God, god	divinity, divine, deity, divination, deify
demo	people	democracy, demagogue, epidemic
dia	through, across, between	diameter, diagonal, dialogue dialect, dialectic, diagnosis, diachronic
dict	speak	predict, verdict, malediction, dictionary, dictate, dictum, diction, indict
dis, dys, dif	away, not, negative	dismiss, differ, disallow, disperse, dissuade, disconnect, dysfunction, disproportion, disrespect, distemper, distaste, disarray, dyslexia
duc, duct	to lead, pull	produce, abduct, product, transducer, viaduct, aqueduct, induct, deduct, reduce, induce
dyn, dyna	power	dynamic, dynamometer, heterodyne, dynamite, dynamo, dynasty
ecto	outside, external	ectomorph, ectoderm, ectoplasm, ectopic, ectothermal
endo	inside, withing	endotoxin, endoscope, endogenous
equi	equal	equidistant, equilateral, equilibrium, equinox, equitable, equation, equator

e, ex	out, away, from	emit, expulsion, exhale, exit, express, exclusive, enervate, exceed, explosion
exter, extra	outside of	external, extrinsic, exterior extraordinary, extra-biblical extracurricular, extrapolate, extraneous
flu, flux	flow	effluence, influence, effluvium, fluctuate, conflu-ence, reflux, influx
flect, flex	to bend	flexible, reflection, deflect, circumflex
graph, gram	to write	polygraph, grammar, biography, graphite, tele-gram, autograph, lithograph, historiography, graphic
hetero	other	heterodox, heterogeneous, heterosexual, hetero-dyne
homo	same	homogenized, homosexual, homonym, homo-phone
hyper	over, above	hyperactive, hypertensive, hyperbolic, hypersen-sitive, hyperventilate, hyperkinetic
hypo	below, less than	hypotension, hypodermic, hypoglycemia, hypoal-lergenic
in, im	not	inviolate, innocuous, intractable, innocent, im-pregnable, impossible
infra	beneath	infrared, infrastructure
inter, intro	between	international, intercept, intermission, interoffice, internal, intermittent, introvert, introduce
intra	within, into	intranet, intracranial, intravenous
jac, ject	to throw	reject, eject, project, trajectory, interject, dejected, inject, ejaculate
mal	bad, badly	malformation, maladjusted, dismal, malady, mal-content, malfeasance, maleficent
mega	great, million	megaphone, megalomaniac, megabyte, megalopo-lis
meso	middle	mesomorph, mesoamerica, mesosphere
meta	beyond, change	metaphor, metamorphosis, metabolism, metahis-torical, metainformation
meter	measure	perimeter, micrometer, ammeter, multimeter, al-timeter
micro	small	microscope, microprocessor, microfiche, microm-eter, micrograph

mis	bad, badly	misinform, misinterpret, mispronounce, misnomer, mistake, misogynist
mit, miss	to send	transmit, permit, missile, missionary, remit, admit, missive, mission
morph	shape	polymorphic, morpheme, amorphous
multi	many	multitude, multipartite, multiply, multipurpose
neo	new	neologism, neonate, neoclassic, neophyte
non	not	nonferrous, nonabrasive, nondescript
omni	all	omnipotent, omnivorous, omniscient
para	beside	paraprofessional, paramedic, paraphrase, parachute
per	through, intensive	permit, perspire, perforate, persuade
peri	around	periscope, perimeter, perigee, periodontal
phon	sound	telephone, phonics, phonograph, phonetic, homophone, microphone
phot	light	photograph, photosynthesis, photon
poly	many	polytheist, polygon, polygamy, polymorphous
port	to carry	porter, portable, report, transportation, deport, import, export
re	back, again	report, realign, retract, revise, regain
retro	backwards	retrorocket, retrospect, retrogression, retroactive
sanct	holy	sanctify, sanctuary, sanction, sanctimonious, sacrosanct
scrib, script	to write	inscription, prescribe, proscribe, manuscript, conscript, scribble, scribe
sect, sec	cut	intersect, transect, dissect, secant, section
semi	half	semifinal, semiconscious, semiannual, semimonthly, semicircle
spect	to look	inspect, spectator, circumspect, retrospect, prospect, spectacle
sub	under, below	submerge, submarine, substandard, subnormal, subvert
super, supra	above	superior, suprarenal, superscript, supernatural, supercede

syn	together	synthesis, synchronous, syndicate
tele	distance, from afar	television, telephone, telegraph, telemetry
theo, the	God	theology, theist, polytheist
therm, thermo	heat	thermal, thermometer, thermocouple, thermodynamic, thermoelectric
tract	to drag, draw	attract, tractor, traction, extract, retract, protract, detract, subtract, contract, intractable
trans	across	transoceanic, transmit, transport, transducer
un	not	uncooked, unharmed, unintended
veh, vect	to carry	vector, vehicle, convection, vehement
vert, vers	to turn	convert, revert, advertise, versatile, vertigo, invert, reversion, extravert, introvert
vita	life	vital, vitality, vitamins, revitalize

Number Prefixes

Prefix	Meaning	Examples
mono, uni	one	monopoly, monotype, monologue, mononucleosis, monorail, monotheist, unilateral, universal, unity, unanimous, uniform
bi, di	two	divide, diverge, diglycerides, bifurcate, biweekly, bivalve, biannual
tri	three	triangle, trinity, trilateral, triumvirate, tribune, trilogy
quat, quad	four	quadrangle, quadruplets
quint, penta	five	quintet, quintuplets, pentagon, pentane, pentameter
hex, ses, sex	six	hexagon, hexameter, sestet, sextuplets
sept	seven	septet, septennial
oct	eight	octopus, octagon, octogenarian, octave
non	nine	nonagon, nonagenarian
dec	ten	decimal, decade, decalogue, decimate
cent	hundred	centennial, century, centipede
mill, kilo	thousand	millennium, kilobyte, kiloton
mega	million	megabyte, megaton, megaflop

giga	billion	gigabyte, gigaflop
tera	trillion	terabyte, teraflop
milli	thousandth	millisecond, milligram, millivolt
micro	millionth	microgram, microvolt
nano	billionth	nanosecond, nanobucks
pico	trillionth	picofarad, picocurie
femto	quadrillionth	femtosecond

Notes

The #1 Rap Study Guide On Planet. **The Official How To Rap Manual** will help take your rhyme skills to unprecedent heights. The Author Jamaal "J-Mill" West has over 17 years in the rap world, and 7yrs in the music industry.

With his record label starting, his book doing well, nationally and internatio- nally, A new EP on Itunes, Rhapsody, Emusic and other online locations, and a huge accomplishment of having one of his songs featured on a game from one of the Top Gaming Companies in the Gaming industry, the time has come for J-Mill to take his place amongst the top talent in The Hip-Hop industry today.

"The Point System that J-Mill has came up with has done wonders for my rap flow"
-L Ninyo Bronx, NY

"The Official How To Rap Manual and How2rap.com has helped me in so many ways. I can go in the studio and lay my lyrics down in one take. It used to take me 5-6 times before I got it down."
-Jackie Girl Pimpstress New Orleans

How2rap.com

Made in the USA
San Bernardino, CA
02 November 2012